Building our house

By

GM Harlow

ISBN 978-1-4467-4947-0

Contents

Introduction

When people tell you that they built their own house, they don't usually mean that. They mean that they supervised the builders, the joiners, the electricians and so on. We were different. We did it all ourselves, with the exception of the plastering, and the construction of the staircase.

When we built our house, from 1976 to 1980, many friends asked me if I would be writing a book about it. At the time I thought not, because it was really quite boring most of the time. That was over thirty years ago, and I have only just begun to see the enormity of what we did. It all seemed natural at the time.

There were no builders, just Hugh and I. The full extent of Hugh's bricklaying experience had been the building of a sandpit for our son in our garden in Wetherby, and a sheltering wall behind it. I had worked as a book-keeper in a house building firm, although of course I had never done any quantity surveying or building!

What really inspired me to write this were the photographs. In recent times many houses in the UK were flooded. I heard the heartbreak of people who had lost such treasures as their photo albums. My heart went out to them, being a very sentimental person. I thought one way to avoid such a disaster might be to upload all the photographs to the internet. I bought a special scanner to scan slides, and another scanner to rapidly scan photos. I made albums of each of my children growing up, and had them made up as 'photo books' by a well known firm on the internet. They are now in their thirties, and I gave them these books as Christmas presents in 2009. So now they each have a pictorial record of their childhood, and I can have more made up should the need arise. I also uploaded all the photos of our wedding and of our son and daughter's weddings.

I then uploaded all of the slides I had taken during the four years of house building, and made up a 'photo book' of many of the slides. It was quite a task to pick out a suitable selection of the slides for the photo book. The uploading and book making process took months, because I had been such a prolific photographer. Then, this year, I decided to write up some detail to go with the photographs of the house building, so here it is!

The Idea

When we were first married, our house was a police house, as Hugh was then a Police Constable, after serving nine years as a soldier. It was actually a council house on an estate in Leeds, controlled by the Watch Committee. Hugh's pay was lessened to pay the rent, and we thought it would be better to move out and try and buy our own house. This was allowed in the Leeds City force, though not in neighbouring forces at that time. We thought we could use Hugh's pay for the mortgage and my pay for the housekeeping. Hugh's uncle lent us £200 for a deposit on a tiny semi in Leeds. To his astonishment we paid him back within three months. However those three months had been crucial, because house prices had risen tremendously due to inflation. This was early 1970.

Two years later, after improving the inside of the house, we sold it at a good profit, and bought a larger semi in Wetherby, Hugh having left the Police for better pay. It was badly in need of renovation and we actually camped out in the front sitting room for the first few months. Just cleaning it was quite a task, and then we had to scrape off layers of paint and wallpaper. In the kitchen there were layers of dirty mats held down by grease. We knocked through a wall from the kitchen into the coal house to extend the kitchen a little. We still had a coal fire but were given a second hand bunker which we put behind the garage.

The Wetherby house was quite a nice house. It was a typical semi-detached house with its bow windows and a fir tree in the front garden. At the rear, beyond our modest back garden, was a field used by a market gardener, so we had a pleasant open outlook.

The Wetherby House

In the photograph you can see our old Morris Minor, which we sold to buy a 'camping' van when our son was two.

We had, what seemed to us, a stiff mortgage. By today's standards it certainly wasn't. In those days the banks and building societies would take only one wage into account when calculating how much we could borrow. We each earned roughly the same when we took out our first mortgage, but like most couples, chose to use Hugh's salary for the mortgage calculation. This meant that we could, if careful, afford the mortgage with only Hugh working, when our son was born.

It was the early seventies, and like most women at that time, I left work to become a full time mum. We always thought that we could save money, having me at home with the time to cook cheaper foods and not needing so many clothes and so on. However, babies are expensive, and we realised that we were on a treadmill like two hamsters in a wheel. We would never be free of the mortgage, and would never be able to afford anything. I had joined a baby and toddler group and we all swapped children's clothing and toys, as they were outgrown. That helped a lot.

Then the field at the back was sold and an estate of new houses appeared, almost overnight. It is amazing how quickly these estates can be built. During the building process we walked around and looked at the foundations and the progress.

Hugh had been trained to work for a pest control firm. He surveyed houses for mortgage applications, and checked for such things as dry rot and woodworm. This took him to many parts of the country. He had been working in Lincolnshire, and he spoke of the wide open spaces there, and the cheapness of the houses and the land. We discussed our financial problems in the evenings, and decided that we could 'get off the hamster wheel' and better ourselves by moving to a cheaper area and building a house ourselves.

Hugh had made a large blackboard for our son, and we used this in the evenings to draw up tentative plans for our new house. First we made a list of what we wanted from our house. We thought three bedrooms would suffice, with an extra reception room that could double as a bedroom. I wanted a good sized kitchen, but not so large that it would be a chore to work in. We decided that we wanted the house to look modest from the outside, so a dormer bungalow seemed a good plan. We were not too bothered about large living rooms, unlike most people, because we were very conscious of the cost of heating. Double glazing was yet to be widely popular. I cannot even recall whether there was such a thing in 1976. So we designed the rooms to be about the same size as in the semi, but with a small extension to the main living room. Actually we eventually failed to build the living room extension in favour of a patio. With these ideas we drew up the plans, first on the black board and then on paper.

We put our house on the market, at a fair price. One thing I hated was that I had to keep showing people round our home. Our son was two years old, and of course there were toys about and so on, and I had to have the house looking spotless all the time.

We asked an estate agent friend, who knew another estate agent in Lincolnshire, to look out for any suitable building plots. Armed with a short list of three, we set off to go and take a look.

One of them was a semi-derelict house with half an acre of land, and a large caravan in which the current owners lived. However, the price would not leave us much cash with which to improve the house. We subsequently realized that we would need to spend thousands on 'underpinning' the house foundations and this put us off.

The second plot was too near a main road. The third looked all right, except that it was very closely between two existing houses. I had envisaged our building venture would be a little more 'out of the way' than this. However, it was in a small village, with a shop next door, and it was only three miles to the nearest town.

By this time we had found a buyer for our Wetherby house. This was a first time buyer with no chain, so we decided to go for it. We bought the plot with the proceeds of the house, and this left us with a large sum, after paying off the Wetherby house mortgage. Inflation had been kind to us, as house prices had risen again since we had bought it. We had made various improvements also which presumably increased its price further, so now we had a tidy profit. Perfect, we thought, we will buy as many of the building materials as possible.

We took our plans to an architect, and asked him to translate them into 'proper' plans, with any changes he thought would be necessary. He didn't change anything, which really surprised us. We were rather disappointed in a way as we felt we had paid quite a lot for our own design. We later discovered that we had not really thought about where the furniture would go, as there were a lot of doors and windows.

The main fault though, was that the hallway was somewhat dark. The architect had envisaged this and had suggested a roof window above the stairs. However, Hugh was very reluctant to 'break' the roof on the north side so it is still a little dark. I suppose we are used to it now.

Meanwhile Hugh had bought a technical book on house building, which was used by apprentices when studying for their diplomas. Hugh called it his 'bible.' I recall that, to my embarrassment, he even told the vicar that it was his bible! He didn't mean it like that really – it was just a turn of phrase with him. This book became very much thumbed. Sadly he gave it away some years ago, and we are now unable to recall its title.

The Caravan

We began to look out for a suitably large caravan in which we could live while we built the house. At that stage we thought it might take two years (!!). Friends knew of our search and pretty soon someone told us about a caravan currently located in a field. We went to look. I thought it was somewhat grotty, but it did have the advantage of a solid fuel stove, which we thought could be an advantage in winter time. The price was also a plus point. We purchased the van and towed it back to the cul de sac using our camping van.

The camping van wasn't a proper camping van but a former mini bus which had belonged to a friend who had his own company at Thorp Arch Trading Estate. He'd used it to transport his staff. Hugh had taken out all the rear seats and made a removable kitchen and table for it. When we'd camped, we'd used a tent to sleep in, and the van for everything else. The summer of 1976 was a wonderful summer and the last holiday we would have for a while. We went to Northumberland near Craster, of the wonderful kippers, then across to Gatehouse of Fleet in Scotland for the second week. It was blue skies and sunshine all the way. Our two year old son loved the beaches and paddling in the sea.

Meanwhile back at the cul-de -sac, we parked the caravan outside our friends' house third door up. No room outside ours as we were in the 'point' of the cul-de sac. Actually all were our friends in the cul de sac. It was a wonderful neighbourhood. We'd had parties where everyone joined in.

We painted the caravan inside and out, put down new lino in the kitchen and some (uprooted from the house) carpet in the living area. It then looked a little more like home and not quite so grotty.

This is the interior before we laid the carpet and lino. As you may be able to see it had gas lamps!

Getting There

One November morning in 1976, we bid farewell to our home, and set off on our big adventure. I was tearful to leave the house as we had been happy there. We'd spent many happy hours 'doing it up' and our son's little room was, I thought, a really nice little nursery.

Our furniture and other belongings were stored in a house belonging to some former cul-de-sac- neighbours who had moved into a very large house in Wetherby. All except our three piece suite which was with my parents. In the caravan we only had room for a few practical clothes, our son's toys, and I brought the Christmas cactus of all things! I thought it would make it seem more like home. We also had various tools in the back of the van.

The journey was uneventful until we reached our new town. There we discovered that the caravan number plate was trailing, so we stopped to fix it. Then the road from town up to our village was the bumpiest of the entire journey! It remains like that to this day.

On arrival at our plot, we found that we were unable to tow the caravan on to the plot, because people had been dumping their garden rubbish all along the front perimeter. All these little hillocks made it impossible to get on the land. The lady in the bungalow next door said we could park on her driveway, which was very kind. She also gave us a cup of tea, and some water to be going on with. Her husband was somewhat surprised when he arrived home. The next day we hailed a passing farmer with a large tractor, and he agreed to pull the van onto the land for us.

Our first task was to make some sort of driveway. We also wanted to remove all the top soil from the building area, so that we could replace it later for the garden. We found a self employed man in a nearby village with a JCB, and asked him to come along and move the top soil, resulting in a hill of topsoil at the bottom of the plot. We also then had a smooth area on which to make the driveway. We obtained some hardcore which was actually road scrapings of used tarmac. This made for a steady surface for the time being. We were able to site the van properly, and made a system of planks from it over all the mud.

November 1976

The logistics

We had to work out how many bricks we would need, and all the rest. Basic maths worked fine, and I ordered the bricks. I knew that the brick company would allow for 10% imperfect bricks. They later gave us 10% extra. Then we also ordered the internal breeze blocks.

It was ridiculously exciting when these things arrived. From this location it is possible to see right down the road toward the town. I remember seeing the brick lorry coming and jumping up and down with excitement like a child.

I almost forgot to take a photo, but here is one with the lorry arriving at our site.

Below is the lorry with the breeze blocks arriving. On this picture you can see how close we are to the neighbours. The caravan is a holiday caravan in their driveway. You can see our Bedford 'camping' van on what was now our driveway and in the foreground is Hugh with our son. As you can see there had been a fall of snow.

Many people asked us why we had begun this venture in November. Well it was simple really. Our house had been on the market since the spring, and we'd only just got the buyer and had all the paper work sorted out. Sadly it isn't so easy to plan these things just when you would like. Not if you are doing it all on a shoe string like us anyway.

We had failed to realise that neighbours would have misgivings about people self-building a house right next door. We would probably not have bought this plot had we considered this at the time. With hindsight it could have been better to lose our first time buyer, and try to sell again next spring instead. The fact that we were trying to rid ourselves of our mortgage meant that we did not wish to spend our money on rented property, which made things somewhat tight.

Finances

We still had money left over from the sale of the house, but we knew that it would not last until the house was finished. Hugh had given up his job in Wetherby, as they would not continue to employ someone who lived so far from the depot at Thorp Arch. Also we thought it would give us a good start if Hugh worked on the house full time for a while. Some of the local people appeared to think that we were on the 'dole.' As it was, we were not on the 'dole' because we didn't qualify, having too much money in the bank, and Hugh had given up his job voluntarily. We were living on our own money.

However, someone from Social Services came round about our son. We gathered that they had been alerted that a child was being kept in unsuitable circumstances. The upshot was that they were satisfied that our rosy cheeked and happy little boy was fine, but that he qualified for free milk, in spite of our savings.

After four months Hugh found a job working on a security force. His previous experience as a Police Constable probably gave him an advantage. The fact that he was on shift work meant that he was home often during the daytime hours when he worked on the house. Unfortunately this gave some people the impression that he was still out of work.

Round about this time we thought perhaps we would complete the house, sell it, and then move back to Wetherby with the proceeds, but minus a mortgage.

Little Life details

Before we left Wetherby, I had made our son a one piece suit from waterproof material. The idea was that if he went to play outside, we put the suit on top of his clothes, with his little Wellingtons. That suit became so caked in mud that it stood up on its own just inside the door!

The neighbour in the bungalow supplied us with water for a couple of days, until the water board came and fixed up a stand pipe for us at the road edge of the plot. We were not allowed to have electricity until we had something to fix it to, so life was primitive.

We took our dirty clothes to the launderette in the nearby town and a large plastic former bread delivery box became our bath. We heated the water in a large kettle on top of the stove, and poured it into the bath. Of course it wasn't deep at all so we had to stand up and wash ourselves, although our son could have a 'normal' bath in it.

The caravan had a chemical 'loo, which we were able to empty into the sewerage manhole cover. One thing about being between two existing houses was that the main drain ran across our property.

So the first task was to build the garage/workshop so that we could have electricity. It still stands and is quite large. There was then a separate room at the back where we fixed up a shower, a flush toilet, and a large sink. We then bought a second hand twin tub washing machine. I still remember doing the washing wearing coat, hat, gloves and large rubber gloves over the top of the woollen ones.

The apex roofs you can see belong to the neighbours.

The workshop/wash house windows were metal ones from an old RAF hut that we'd been given in Wetherby.

We wanted to purchase the wooden window and door frames for the house, and bought another old caravan from the neighbour with the bungalow, in which to store them. Once the workshop was finished we retrieved all our furniture and belongings from the friend in Wetherby and stored them in the workshop section. The three piece suite stayed with my parents for the time being.

We bought all the roof timbers, and these we stacked in the garden. We stood them on bricks which had planks across, and placed pegs between the timbers with the idea of allowing them to season more than they were. It seemed that most wood was rather new these days and liable to twist and bend in use. We wanted to avoid this.

From some of the pictures you can see how close we are to the neighbours, and perhaps understand why we were not too popular with our self build. Had we hired a firm of builders who would have built the house in a matter of months, it perhaps would have been different. Still, we had committed ourselves by then, so heigh ho we carried on and kept calm!

Then to the house

Once the workshop was finished, and washhouse operational, we at last measured out the house.

Hugh became impatient with me as I wanted to take photos, and was almost too excited to hold on to the other end of the tape properly! We got it all marked out with wooden pegs and string, and then checked it again at least twice over.

I kept imagining standing in my kitchen, walking through the house and so on!

We then dug the footings by hand. Footings consist of trenches in which to begin building the walls. We'd bought a second hand cement mixer from a relative who had built his own garage. However, we decided it was cost effective to use ready mixed cement when large amounts were needed. So there was great excitement (on my part) when we saw the cement wagon coming up the road. A friend had offered to help, because the cement would have to be moved into position before it began to set. The wagon poured the cement in to the footings nearest to the roadside at different positions, and we began shovelling like mad, to spread it all along the footing trenches. A couple of hours or so later, it was all in position and we were absolutely 'Christmas Crackered.'

More on lifestyle

By this time, I had found a playgroup in the nearby town which took children aged two and half provided they were potty trained. I dropped our son off at 9.30am and collected him again at 11.30am on two days a week. The first few times I stayed outside the door listening, because he had cried when he saw that I was leaving. However, it was just as the playgroup leader had said; once I had gone he was fine! This gave me more time to help Hugh with the house building, as well as the benefit to our son of being with other small children and learning to play alongside others.

There was another small boy in the village, of our son's age, and the two became regular playmates.

There was also a little girl next door, bungalow side, who was a few years older, and she too liked to play with our son.

Pretty soon we had quite a little group of children coming round to play, and the head teacher of the village school who lived next door but one, told us she would warn them in school about the dangers of playing in sand and so on. We said we thought probably they gained from learning through play, and yes we actually kept them off the sand anyway because it was building sand which stains clothing. We had used an old tractor tyre to make a sand pit for our son with some clean sand.

As the plot sloped, we had to 'step' the foundations, to keep the house level. This means that the house is higher off the ground at the lower end, going down the lane, and there are steps up to the back door. We minimised the back door steps when we built a porch there, on a plinth which is several inches high.

Once these were in place, the whole of the base needed to be filled with hardcore. We had ordered for two lorry loads initially to see how it went. Hugh was out at work when the first load arrived. He'd got a job which involved shift work, so that he had often time off during the daylight hours in which to work on the house. However, this time he was at work.

By this time I was pregnant with our second child. We hadn't wanted to have too big a gap between them, and our son would be four and a quarter years old when this one was born. We had been so optimistic about how long everything would take, but clearly it was all taking longer as Hugh was in full time work. We'd been here over eighteen months already, and our son was now almost four.

I was very eager for the house to progress, so when the lorry dropped off the first load in the driveway, I used the wheelbarrow to begin filling the foundations with it. Our son had his own little wheelbarrow and helped me! I thought that, even being pregnant, I would be all right if I didn't over fill the barrow. By the time the wagon came back with the second load, the first load was all in the foundations. The driver was amazed to learn that my son and I had done this. Of course there are no photographs of our doing that, because there was no-one else there to take them! Needless to say we didn't manage to get the second load in, as we were tired, son was bored, and it was time to get tea ready!

The next task was to put down damp proof membrane everywhere and fill with cement. Once again we had the cement wagon deliver fresh cement. We then had to tamp down the cement. We held a long plank edge to the cement, one of us at each side, and tamped away until it was all flat and well bedded in. We had done this earlier with the workshop so had some practice behind us.

Later it rained, but we knew that it didn't matter at this stage. It was better if the cement took time to 'go off' apparently rather than do so too quickly.

Next day it was really wonderful to walk on the floors of our new home. I kept imagining baking in the kitchen, and sitting in the living room and so on. You would have thought it was a huge mansion rather than a very modest little house!

Then Hugh began to build the walls up. I sorted out bricks into cracked, chipped and perfect. The cracked ones were discarded and stored away at the bottom of the plot. The chipped ones were put by to be used on the insides of the chimney etc, the perfect ones were used on the house walls. I used to keep a supply by where Hugh was working. I couldn't carry a hod full as a real 'brickie's labourer' would, but I was able to supply sufficient to keep him going, as he was slower than a real bricklayer, and in any case was at work full time on shift work. I placed out little stacks at intervals when he was away at work, so that he could just get straight on, after I'd mixed him some cement. Often he mixed the cement himself if I was busy with our son.

Once the foundation floor cement was totally set, Hugh began to build up the foundation walls.

The walls went up very quickly. By this time we had all the window frames stored in the second caravan we'd bought from the bungalow neighbour. These of course had to be fitted in when building up the walls. We had a bit of trouble with the supplier because we had wanted the windows to mirror each other at the back of the house i.e. the opening window on the opposite sides so that it would look symmetrical. We sent one of the windows back to be exchanged, but sadly the same one came back. Presumably it wasn't possible to get one the other way round, or perhaps they hadn't understood what we meant? Anyway we gave up and these windows are still in place as I write.

Hugh had started to do up a small boat for the friend who'd helped with the cement earlier, and you can see it in the foreground of the photograph below.
The caravan on the right is the one in which the window frames were stored.

Photo shows window frames propped up ready. The caravan on the left is the one we were living in. Hugh is with an elderly gent from the village who had come around to 'inspect' the progress.

It was hot on some days in the summer, and here is a rare photo of me, placing sorted bricks ready for Hugh to use. Although scantily clad here, I normally had proper shoes on my feet and gloves on my hands! This is just by the front door. Usually I am the photographer which is why I rarely appear!

By the back door. This was before we built the side porch and there are four steps up to the door.

Rolling out the ground at the back that was to become our garden.

Work stopped in the winter. Here is the front of the house with the pile of building sand.

This is the view across the road which is entirely blocked.

After the snow we carried on. Our son liked to help.

Breeze blocks form the inner walls.

Our bungalow neighbour had planted a leylandii hedge between us. In the next photo it is very tiny. The hedge is still there as I write. It is now known as 'bird city' and very dense and tall which we like. However, hedges are not to everyone's taste. You can see that we were growing our own potatoes on the right. The tower scaffolding was used by the children as a climbing frame.

We bought another caravan so that my parents could come and stay with us for a week or so in the summer. They didn't mind caravan life at all as they had a little wooden cabin in the Yorkshire Dales where they took many holidays. This was a similar situation to them.

It was especially useful to have my father there to baby sit our son, on the night Hugh had to take me to hospital to give birth to our daughter. I was offered a week in the maternity home and accepted this gladly. We had only the shower, and it is really good to be able to take baths after a birth. Also it was great to have such a good rest. Our son had grown some flowers in a little plot that we'd given him, and he picked them all to bring to me in the maternity home. I was so overcome that I burst into tears, much to his consternation! We all had to reassure him that I was crying because I was so happy.

Hugh used sheets from the now defunct store caravan to build an extension on the living caravan, so that we had more room with the new baby.

Hugh constructed the roof himself rather than buy ready made struts. This way he could make it just as we wanted. The Vulcan bombers from Scampton used to fly over our house, which was on their flight path for the runway. They were so low you could see the pilot sometimes, especially if you were sitting on a roof joist as Hugh was one day. He waved to the pilot who then wobbled the wings slightly after he passed over, by way of a wave! Unless of course Hugh's sudden movement had startled him – big bird on a roof?

Since we had been the gap between two houses, presumably the pilots must have noticed the house being built over the four years.

Things seemed a lot quicker than when we first started. It took such a long time to get the house off the ground! I suppose because the foundations are so very important, and we had to be sure that we had everything right. Also it was a lot of physical work for the two of us at that stage.

Pretty soon Hugh had the felt on the roof and the strips of wood that would hold it down and carry the tiles. Once again I was a labourer, going up and down the ladder with tiles for Hugh. We got them stacked at intervals so that Hugh could just get on with it. The baby was now three months old, and it was a case of taking up tiles between feeds, nappy changes and all the washing that goes with babies, plus our washing too. People used to say how easy my life must be, living in a caravan because the housework must be minimal!

We were tiling the roof on Christmas Day that year.

Now the house was a reality, but it still took another two years to have it ready for us to move in.

Hugh began work on the fireplace in the living room, and found a friend from work who was actually a plasterer, but currently on shift work. This plasterer came in his off shift time, which coincided with Hugh's off shift time, and he plastered while Hugh laboured for him. First they put up cement render on the breeze blocks which lined the walls. This was heavy work, but it did give us really strong and sound deadening walls. Then they plastered over that. The exceptions were the upstairs 'stool' walls. Being a dormer bungalow we have sloping ceilings upstairs, and the small walls are just plaster board here. We made openings and lined the remaining space to create extra storage cupboards.

As they finished each room, I painted it twice. We had bought very large tins of cheap white emulsion, as we knew that the first coat would sink into the plaster. Our daughter was crawling about by now, and our son was at school. Unfortunately it was hard to concentrate on putting paint on the walls and watch a small child at the same time. Therefore some of the rooms have great splodges of paint in the middle where I had placed the paint pot, and our daughter had accidentally toppled it over or otherwise made free with the paint. She was really too young to know any better just then. The floor boards were just hardboard sheets, so we hadn't planned to make anything of them.

The next picture is taken from the rear of the plot towards the house. You can see our caravan with the extension on, and our vegetable plot in the foreground.

Spring 1980

Eventually, when our daughter was two years old and our son was six, we moved in to our house. It was August 1980.

1980

We were busy but happy. There was a lot to do. We took all of our possessions out of the workshop and moved them into the house. It was really strange unpacking things we hadn't seen for four years. It was like greeting old friends, although there were some things we wondered why we'd kept. The entire outside had to be sorted out too. Two old caravans to dispose of and all the mess associated with building. We were able to sell the one we'd bought for my parents to stay in. However, the one we had lived in was not saleable because of the extension we'd built on it. We scrapped it with mixed feelings. Happy to be in the house and see it go, but it had been our home for four years too.

We moved in August 1980

The picture below shows the front in 1980. You can see the shop next door on the far left. It is now (2010) part of the bungalow, as the shop closed years ago.

We planted more leylandii up by the house, which you can see in the photo below, and also we were planting the lawn which you can see marked out here.

Below are the children in the garden with pet rabbit and still with the tyre sand pit. The original leylandii was growing tall and thick by then as can be seen on the photo. We had fenced off the lower half of the garden for vegetables.

Here is the rear of the house. The children were using an old tarpaulin and blankets to make dens.

1981

Conclusions

Building the house ourselves certainly got rid of the mortgage, and we haven't had one since. We did take out a loan to put in the central heating, after we'd been in the house for a year, but that was paid off within two years.

We have a much nicer house than we would otherwise have had, and have settled in here very well. We have been very much better off having no mortgage all these years, and the whole experience has enriched the quality of our lives.

We had not anticipated that people would be hostile to our venture, and this was a real shock to us, having come from such a friendly neighbourhood. We were somewhat naïve in this respect. It ought to have been obvious to us that an extended building time in a plot right next door would be unwelcome. Over the years we have become part of the community with active roles within it.

If you want to build your dream house, please consider that the neighbours and neighbourhood will make a huge difference. If at all possible, build your house some distance from any others

We are very happy here and are much better off than we would have been had we not built the house ourselves. It is a venture to be recommended.

Above photo taken in the garden, about 1991. The mature hedge, at 7 feet in height, created a really good garden atmosphere.

A close up of the wild life pond. The children used to bring newts, frogspawn, fish and water snails. As far as we know the descendants of these are still here.

The front of the house in 2009.

www.ingramcontent.com/pod-product-compliance
Ingram Content Group UK Ltd.
Pitfield, Milton Keynes, MK11 3LW, UK
UKHW041834200726
13854UKWH00003BA/1125

9 781446 763964